The CHRISTMAS Book

How to Have the Best Christmas Ever

Juliana Foster

SCHOLASTIC INC.

New York   Toronto   London   Auckland   Sydney
Mexico City   New Delhi   Hong Kong   Buenos Aires

Library of Congress Cataloging-in-Publication data is available.

ISBN-13: 978-0-545-06443-9
ISBN-10: 0-545-06443-0

First published in Great Britain in 2007 by Michael O'Mara Books Limited.

Text copyright © 2007 by Michael O'Mara Books Limited.
Cover design by Angie Allison
Cover illustration by David Woodroffe

12 11 10 9 8 7 6 5 4 3 2   8 9 10 11 12 13/0

Printed in the U.S.A.
First American edition, October 2008

To Henry

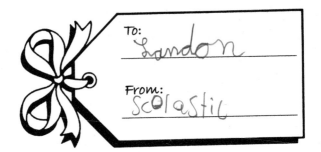

TO: Landon

From: Scolastic

Contents

Introduction

Christmas is a time for peace on Earth and goodwill to all. It is a time for family and friends, for sitting in front of a crackling fire on cold, crisp days, enjoying the spicy aroma of apple cider while admiring your Christmas tree adorned with twinkling lights.

It is also a time for family feuding, overdraft charges and piles of bills, pretending to like bad gifts, turkeys that refuse to defrost, drowning in a mountain of wrapping paper, and indigestion.

Whether you're one of life's Scrooges — turning off all the lights and hiding behind the sofa when the carolers come calling, content with pizza for Christmas dinner, and doing all your Christmas shopping at the local thrift store — or whether you throw yourself into the spirit of the season with gusto, a merry "Ho! Ho! Ho!" escaping from your lips at every opportunity, we all need a little help at Christmas.

Now you can learn how to have the best Christmas ever without breaking a sweat. You'll find out how to wrap those awkwardly shaped presents, how to choose and care for a tree, how to cope with cooking a meal large enough to feed a small town for a week, how to keep the family entertained when all there is on the TV is yet another *Christmas Story* rerun—it's all to be found within these pages. Full of jokes, tips, trivia, and fake thank-you letters, this book is all you'll need to get you through the ups and downs of the holiday season.

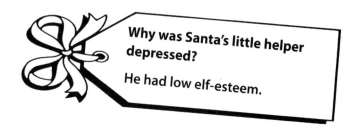

Why was Santa's little helper depressed?

He had low elf-esteem.

How to Host a Christmas Party: Part One

So you've decided to throw caution to the wind and host your own Christmas bash, and you want the occasion to be a memorable one. Needless to say, this isn't as simple as laying out some cheese on toothpicks and leaving your guests to fend for themselves. Read on for some great tips on how to make sure your party is the one everybody is talking about this year.

Invitations

If you don't want to spend the evening sitting by yourself, surrounded by enough food to feed an army for a month, make sure you send out your invitations at least three weeks before the event.

Be realistic when it comes to your guest list. How many people can you comfortably accommodate? There's nothing worse than a room crammed full of hot, sweaty guests all shouting at the tops of their lungs to make themselves heard while struggling to get anywhere near the food and drink. What is your budget? If you don't have much to spend, stick to a more intimate gathering of close friends and family. Be aware that inevitably someone will call at the last minute to ask whether he or she can bring his or her brother/aunt/new boyfriend, so consider this when deciding on your guest list. Ask people to RSVP and include your phone number and/or e-mail address on your invitations. A few days before the party, you should contact anyone who hasn't replied to confirm whether he or she will be attending.

Invite your immediate neighbors. If you don't get along with them, they probably won't come anyway, but they will appreciate the thought and will be less likely to complain about the noise! If you're adamant about not inviting them, at least warn them that you will be hosting a party and apologize in advance for the inconvenience.

It's always better to mail out invitations rather than sending a group e-mail. People will appreciate the extra care taken and are more likely to RSVP if there is a card sitting on their mantel reminding them to do so. If you do decide to send a group e-mail, send it to yourself and bcc ("blind

4

carbon copy") your guests, so that their inboxes are not suddenly filled up with irritating "reply to all" messages. Along with the obvious information — date, time, your address, etc. — include directions (if your home is difficult to find), available parking spots, dress code (if any — see below), phone numbers of a couple of local cab companies, and perhaps even details of some local hotels for those guests who may need to travel to attend your party.

Themes

Having a theme for your party can be a great icebreaker and allows you to be creative with your decorations. Costumes can be fun, but remember that not everyone enjoys dressing up, and you certainly don't want to force your guests to spend a lot of money renting costumes. If you do decide on

a masquerade party, pick a theme that people can dress for easily using items they will already have in their closets, such as the seventies, rock 'n' roll, or the Roaring Twenties. Color themes are a good alternative to costumes. How about a Christmassy red-and-green theme, or glamorous black-and-white? Or simply ask everyone to wear a hat. The results can be hilarious!

Preparing your house

Even if you think your guests are the most well-behaved people on the planet, a little too much Christmas spirit can mean breakages and spills. You won't enjoy your party if you're constantly worrying about your precious possessions, so pack away that Persian rug and the Meissen tableware in an off-limits room — you can show them off some other time. Have a dustpan and broom and a few cloths and cleaning materials ready so you can quickly deal with any disasters.

If necessary, rearrange your furniture so that people have room to move around and can boogie down if they wish. If you're worried about people spilling drinks on your sofas, toss a few inexpensive throws over them.

Set up a table in the main party room where you can lay out food and drink. One of your jobs as host is to pass these around, but you don't want to be doing that all night long. If you've got the space, it's a good idea to have various plates of snacks scattered around the room on small tables so your guests don't have to line up for a handful of chips.

Put up some signs pointing out where the bathroom is, where to leave coats, and which rooms are off-limits. Ensure you have plenty of toilet paper, clean hand towels, and soap in the bathroom.

Your trash can will fill up quickly. Have a fresh trash bag in it, and keep some spares in the bottom of the can so you don't have to go searching around for extras when one gets filled up. Have a couple of large cardboard boxes ready somewhere out of the way. You can fill these with bottles and other recyclables.

Finally, give your house a good cleaning! You may think that your guests won't notice that dubious-looking ring around your bathtub, but they will.

How to Have a
Green Christmas

It is estimated that each person in the United States produces more than four pounds of garbage every day! At Christmas, our waste production increases as we eat more, drink more, and spend our hard-earned cash on cards and gifts. But there are ways you can lessen the impact you have on the environment without missing out on your annual holiday fun.

Responsible gift giving

Try to avoid buying presents that use disposable parts or that will only last for a week before breaking. Check that any battery-powered gizmos you plan to give can use rechargeable batteries and, if necessary, purchase them separately to be included with your gift. Always look for greener alternatives. For example, a coffee machine with a washable filter is more environmentally friendly than one with a disposable one. Buy products made from recycled materials whenever possible. Check the Internet for possible items. Always buy recycled and recyclable wrapping paper.

Gift cards are great environmentally friendly gifts, as they allow the recipient to choose something he or she actually wants and will use.

Trees and decorations

Check with your local government to see if your town has a program in place to dispose of old trees in an environmentally friendly way. These trees are often composted to produce mulch. Or consider buying a tree with roots that can be replanted in your yard or kept in a pot for next year. Although fake trees are more often than not made from plastics, they last for years and are more or less environmentally sound.

Don't buy cheap, easily breakable decorations. Look for more expensive, durable versions, and fill in the gaps by making your own out of scrap or edible materials (see pages 59 and 60 for some inspiration).

Food and drink

Avoid products that are packaged in a lot of unnecessary wrapping and buy goods that come in large bottles or cartons, rather than many smaller containers of the same product. Invest in some sturdy canvas shopping bags or reuse old plastic ones when you go to the supermarket.

Travel

If you are traveling over Christmas — or people are traveling to you — take responsibility for organizing car pools whenever possible. It'll minimize your impact on the environment and it will be much easier to find parking.

Christmas cards

Consider pruning your Christmas card list and sending fewer this year. You can always send an electronic card or email message instead. If you are sending cards, make sure that they are made from recycled materials. Keep a few of your more attractive Christmas cards to cut up and use as gift tags next year.

Christmas Traditions:
SANTA CLAUS

The fat, jolly man who delivers toys to all good children in just one night is known by many different names throughout the world. In English-speaking countries he is most commonly referred to as Santa Claus or Father Christmas. The name *Santa Claus* comes from the Dutch *Sinterklaas* or *Sint Nicolaas*. Saint Nicholas was born in the third century in a part of Greece that is now Turkey. He devoted his life to helping the sick and needy, especially children, and was eventually made bishop of the city of Myra, which no longer exists. He was venerated throughout Europe and the date of December 6, said to be the day on which he died, was dedicated to him. From the thirteenth century onward, it became customary for bishops to hand out small gifts to children on this day. In many countries, December 6 is still the day on which Christmas presents are exchanged.

In early seventeenth-century England, as a show of resistance to the Puritan disapproval of traditional Christmas festivities, the spirit of Christmas was personified in the shape of a fat, bearded man dressed in green fur-lined robes, thus giving rise to Father Christmas. He was also known as Sir Christmas or Lord Christmas, although he was not yet associated with gift giving or children.

It was in North America that the modern image of Santa Claus was born, as colonists merged the legends of Saint Nicholas and Father Christmas. In his *History of New York* (1809), Washington Irving translated *Sinterklaas* as "Santa Claus." This figure was given further shape by the classic poem "A Visit from Saint Nicholas," better known today as "The Night Before Christmas," which was first published in a New York newspaper in 1823. It was this poem that gave rise to the legend of Santa's reindeer.

Contrary to legend, it was not the Coca-Cola company's famous Christmas advertising campaigns of the thirties that first introduced Santa's traditional red costume. The modern depiction of Santa in red was actually started in 1885 when a Christmas card designed by Boston printer Louis Prang went on sale.

True Christmas Stories: The Tale of the Festive Pants

A long and most unusual feud between brothers-in-law Roy Collette and Larry Kunkel began in 1964 when Larry was given a pair of moleskin pants by his mother. Larry didn't think much of the pants, and so he wrapped them up and gave them to Roy that Christmas. Unimpressed by his brother-in-law's thrifty re-gifting, Roy waited until the following Christmas and gave them back.

The annual pants exchange became a family tradition and for a few years they were given back and forth in this manner until Roy decided to up the ante. That Christmas, Larry received the pants as usual, except this time they were stuffed into a 3-foot-long metal tube. From then on, Roy and Larry would compete with each other every year to see who could come up with the most unusual wrapping method. The aim was to be able to remove the pants without damaging them beyond repair, and they agreed that the contest would only end when the pants were no more.

For twenty-five years, the pants were subjected to some rather ingenious wrapping methods, which included stuffing them into a coffee can that was then soldered shut and placed inside a larger container filled with concrete, mounting them inside a double-glazed window with a twenty-year guarantee, putting them in a 600-pound safe that was then soldered shut, and locking them in the glove compartment of an abandoned car, which was then crushed into a 3-foot-square cube.

Amazingly, the pants were extricated undamaged every time until their sad demise in 1989, when Larry had the idea of trying to encase them in 10,000 pounds of glass. Tragically, even these hardiest of pants proved unable to withstand the stresses of molten glass and the contest — along with the pants — finally came to an end.

What do you get if you cross a snowman and a shark?

Frostbite.

Mail your packages early so the post office can lose them in time for Christmas.
— JOHNNY CARSON

Gift Wrapping Made Easy: Part One

Everyone loves to see a pile of beautifully wrapped presents under the tree on Christmas morning. But often a lack of time coupled with an awkwardly shaped item can make gift wrapping a frustrating chore. If the thought of wrestling with wrapping paper fills you with despair, fret no more. Follow this handy guide to ensure your gifts are always perfectly presented.

Some tips

❊ Don't leave your wrapping until the last minute; wrap your gifts as you buy them. If you're one of those people who makes a mad dash to the store with your list just before closing time on Christmas Eve, turn to the sections on gift buying (see page 36) and plan ahead this year.

❊ Boxes are easier to wrap than oddly shaped gifts, so save square and rectangular containers of various sizes throughout the year, fill them with layers of colored tissue paper, and pop in those hard-to-wrap presents.

❊ Gather everything you'll need to wrap your gifts before you start, including the paper (use recycled paper whenever possible), scissors, tape, and perhaps a ruler — and make sure that you work on a large, flat surface.

❄ Use lots of small strips of tape to secure your wrapping rather than a few longer strips. This will make your package look much neater. Tear off a few strips before you start wrapping and line them up along the edge of the surface you will be working on.

❄ Don't forget to remove any price tags before you wrap!

❄ Make sure you stick on a gift tag or label each present before you move on to the next so you don't forget which is which.

How to wrap a box — beautifully

1. Although this may sound straightforward, it takes a little extra skill to make your gift look special. Using the right amount of paper for your box is crucial. The paper should be wide enough to cover about two-thirds of the height of the box. To get the right length, wrap a ribbon around the box to measure its girth, add 2 inches, and use it as a guide when cutting the paper. If you're not very handy with scissors, use a ruler and pencil to mark where you need to cut, or make folds in the paper.

2. Open up the paper in front of you with the printed side facing down and lay the box on it, top down. Bring one lengthwise edge of paper up and tape it to the side of the box. Make a hem along the opposite edge of the

paper by folding it over about an inch, then bring it up so that it overlaps the first edge and tape it down. Make sure that the paper is very tightly wrapped around the box.

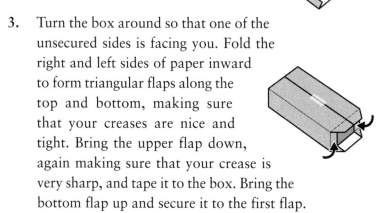

3. Turn the box around so that one of the unsecured sides is facing you. Fold the right and left sides of paper inward to form triangular flaps along the top and bottom, making sure that your creases are nice and tight. Bring the upper flap down, again making sure that your crease is very sharp, and tape it to the box. Bring the bottom flap up and secure it to the first flap.

4. Repeat step 3 on the other side and turn your perfectly wrapped gift right-side up. Ta-da!

How to wrap a tube or cylinder

The easiest way to wrap presents that are cylindrical is to use tissue paper and ribbon:

1. Cut a piece of paper that is a few inches longer than the tube on both ends and wide enough to wrap around the tube a few times.

2. Lay the tissue paper in front of you, printed side down, and place the tube in the center but a few inches above one of the edges.

3. Bring the edge of the paper up and tape it to the tube. Then simply roll the tube along the rest of the paper, making sure that it is tightly wrapped. Tape down the other edge.

4. Twist the paper at both open ends so the gift is sealed inside, and secure the twists with ribbon. If you pull the ends of the ribbon over the blunt edge of a scissor blade in the direction of the ribbon's natural curl, the ribbon will curl tightly and look more decorative.

December 25,
1223

Saint Francis of Assisi assembles the first Nativity scene in Greccio, Italy.

Some Unusual Places to Hide Presents from Prying Kids

❄ In the oven

❄ Up the chimney (though this may provide an authentic present-arriving-from-Santa scenario on Christmas morning)

❄ In the vegetable drawer in the fridge (most kids never go near one)

❄ Underneath the cat

❄ Inside the turkey

❄ Under the patio

❄ On top of the tree

❄ On the mantel

❄ Behind your back

Christmas Traditions:

CHRISTMAS CARDS

Although religiously themed prints made by wood engravers date back to the Middle Ages, the Christmas card is a relatively recent tradition. The widespread exchange of homemade Christmas cards began in Britain in 1840, with the introduction of the first postal service, the Penny Post. The man who played a key role in setting up the Penny Post, Sir Henry Cole, commissioned London artist John Calcott Horsley to produce the first commercially printed Christmas card in 1843. One thousand copies of the card, which depicted a family party and scenes of the poor being clothed and fed, with the inscription "A merry Christmas and a happy New Year to you," were placed on sale. The tradition took off over the next few years as printing methods improved and, by 1860, large numbers were being produced and mailed in Europe. In 1875, lithographer Louis Prang became the first printer to produce Christmas cards in the United States. Today, approximately 2.2 billion Christmas cards are mailed each year.

Famous People Born on Christmas Day

Sir Isaac Newton, scientist (1642)

Pope Pius VI (1717)

Clara Barton, nurse (1821)

Conrad Hilton, hotelier (1887)

Humphrey Bogart, actor (1899)

Howard Hughes, businessman, film director, and aviator (1905)

Cab Calloway, band leader (1907)

Jimmy Buffet, singer (1946)

Sissy Spacek, actress (1949)

Annie Lennox, singer (1954)

Dido, singer (1971)

Santa's Rules

It seems that even Santa needs some basic rules by which to conduct himself. Jenny Zinc, an employee for a U.S. temping agency that has trained and supplied Santas to department stores for more than thirty years, sums up the most important tenets of Santa etiquette as follows:

Santa is even-tempered.

Santa does not hit children over the head who kick him.

Santa uses the term "folks" rather than "Mommy" and "Daddy" because of all the broken homes.

Santa does not borrow money from store employees.

Santa wears a good deodorant.

Christmas Traditions:

STOCKINGS

The practice of hanging up stockings can be traced back to pre-Christian times. Germanic folklore tells of the god Odin's annual Yuletime hunting party. Children would leave out their shoes filled with straw or sugar for Odin's flying horse, and Odin would reward them by leaving small gifts in exchange. Later on, the practice was linked with Saint Nicholas. The story goes that a nobleman with three daughters had fallen on hard times and was unable to give his daughters dowries so that they could be married. Saint Nicholas wanted to help but also remain anonymous, so he threw some gold coins down the chimney. They landed in the girls' stockings that had been hung by the fire to dry.

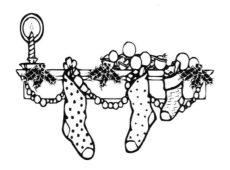

Alternative Uses for Brussels Sprouts

For many, the brussels sprout is a thing of beauty and joy, a delicious and nutritious vegetable without which Christmas dinner just wouldn't be the same. For others, it is Satan's vegetative representative on Earth. If you are of the latter persuasion and would go to any length not to have to actually eat one, here are some alternative uses:

❄ Dip a handful in melted chocolate and place them in an empty box of chocolates, ready to be presented to your least favorite relative.

❄ No white Christmas this year? Never mind. Have a mock snowball fight using the little green veggies instead. You'll be smelling of sprouts for weeks.

❄ Thread a dozen or so together and make a wonderful alternative to the classic pearl necklace.

❄ Leave a plate out for Santa instead of the usual cookies and milk—he could do with losing a few pounds. Be prepared for some disappointment when it comes to opening your presents, though.

❄ Draw the numbers 1 to 49 on them with a Magic Marker and place them in a hat for a novel way to pick your lottery numbers.

✻ Teach yourself how to juggle with them.

✻ Sprinkle them with glitter and dangle them from the Christmas tree—they make great decorations. For a couple of days, at least.

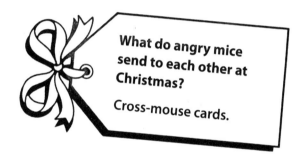

What do angry mice send to each other at Christmas?

Cross-mouse cards.

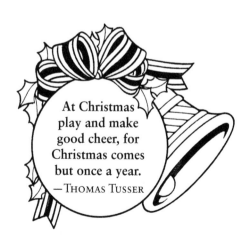

At Christmas play and make good cheer, for Christmas comes but once a year.
—Thomas Tusser

Thank You Very Much . . .

Dear   [name of stingy relative],

Thank you so much for your very generous check. It's great that you refuse to be pressured by the ridiculously stringent gift-giving rules of etiquette.

Despite our intimate family connection, I would hate for you to put yourself to the trouble of hunting down and purchasing a more personal gift. I regret that I was unable not to "spend it all at once," as by the time I had purchased this thank-you card, there was only just enough money left for the bus fare home.

Yours sincerely,

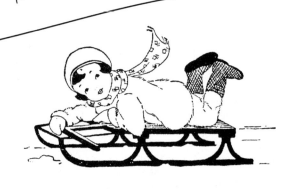

Christmas Dinner

Preparing Christmas dinner is a bit like planning a military operation. If you're going for the traditional turkey with all the trimmings, you need to make sure you're properly organized. The trick is to plan ahead as much as possible so that you're not rushing around trying to do a hundred things at once at the last minute. Prepare as much as you can before Christmas morning and draw up a detailed timetable to remind you when you should be doing what. Of course, menus will vary, and cooking times will depend on the quantities you are serving, but below is a handy timetable that can be used as a rough guide to help make Christmas Day as stress-free as possible.

The week before

❄ If you're making your own sauces, now is the time to start doing so. Cranberry sauce is easy to prepare and will keep for a year if you store it in the freezer. Make a large batch and set some aside for the next big family dinner.

❄ If you like to serve some stuffing separately, prepare and cook it now, in a freezer-proof oven dish, and freeze.

❄ Make your pies and store them in the freezer, ready to be reheated on Christmas Day.

I stopped believing in Santa Claus when I was six. Mother took me to see him in a department store and he asked for my autograph.

— SHIRLEY TEMPLE

Two days before

❄ If you're cooking a frozen turkey, remove it from the freezer now, so that there is no last-minute panic. Being faced with a half-defrosted turkey floating in the bathtub is not a great start to Christmas morning. When it is fully defrosted, keep the turkey in the fridge.

Christmas Eve

❄ Prepare the brussels sprouts so that they are ready for boiling the next day.

❄ Remove the precooked stuffing from the freezer to defrost overnight.

❄ If you're cooking the stuffing in the turkey, prepare the mixture and leave it in the fridge overnight.

❄ Remove the giblets from the turkey and prepare the stock for the gravy. Store it in an airtight container in the fridge overnight.

❄ Sharpen your preparation and carving knives.

❄ Set the table.

❄ First thing in the morning, remove the turkey from the fridge and leave it out, covered, so that it reaches room temperature.

Christmas Day

The following timetable is for a 14-pound turkey. If your turkey is a different size, adjust the timing as necessary.

7:45 A.M. Preheat the oven to 425°F. Get some butter out of the fridge and give it a quick blast in the microwave to soften it. Stuff the turkey, rub it all over with the melted butter, and season it. Wrap the turkey in foil.

8:15 A.M. Put the turkey in the oven. Peel your potatoes and parsnips and place them in cold water until you are ready to cook them.

9:00 A.M. Turn the oven temperature down to 325°F.

12:30 P.M. Turn the oven temperature up to 400°F. Remove the turkey from the oven and take it out of its foil. Baste well and return to the oven. Keep basting regularly. If you are serving the separate, precooked stuffing, cover the oven dish with foil and place it at the bottom of the oven.

12:45 P.M. Place some oil or fat in a roasting tray and put in the oven. Parboil the potatoes for 10 minutes, then drain them well.

1:00 P.M. Transfer the potatoes to the roasting tray and return to the oven. Add some oil to another roasting tray and place in the oven.

1:15 P.M. Check the turkey is cooked through by inserting a skewer into the thickest part of the thigh. If the juices run clear, it's done. If they are pinkish, cook the turkey for a little longer. Once it is cooked through, remove the turkey from the oven, put it on a warm plate, and cover it with foil. Turn the oven temperature up to 450°F. Remove the potatoes and drain off the fat, then place them on the highest shelf of the oven. Put the parsnips in the second roasting tray and return to the middle shelf of the oven. Heat up your preprepared stock and use it to make your gravy. Check the seasoning and place it to one side.

1:45 P.M. Boil the brussels sprouts. Reheat your gravy and gently warm through any additional sauces. From now on keep a close eye on your sauces and vegetables and transfer them to serving dishes as soon as they are ready to serve.

2:00 P.M. Dinner is served! Before you sit down to eat, turn down the oven to 350°F and put in the pies to warm them up.

A Very Veggie Christmas

Catering for vegetarian guests or family members doesn't have to be a chore. With a bit of thought and planning ahead, you can easily accommodate them without adding too much to your workload, and they'll appreciate your thoughtfulness. Consider the following points:

❄ Talk to your vegetarian guest before you plan your vegetarian menu. Some vegetarians love meat substitutes; others can't stand the taste and texture of anything resembling meat. Make sure you ask whether they are vegetarian or vegan (vegans avoid dairy products and eggs as well as meat).

❄ Many foods that don't contain meat may still contain animal products. Some desserts contain gelatin, and animal rennet is often used in cheese. Check the food packaging carefully if you are unsure whether something is suitable.

❄ You don't have to cook an entirely separate meal. Your vegetarian guests will be more than happy to share your vegetable side dishes. Just make sure you keep all your vegetables away from any meat and cook them in vegetable fat. Choose a meat-free stuffing that everyone will enjoy, and be sure to cook some of it outside of the turkey.

✳ Health food stores and some supermarkets stock excellent ready-made vegetarian options, so there's no need to slave away in the kitchen any more than you already are. If you do want to go to the trouble of cooking something yourself, opt for something original, such as a chestnut bourguignon pie. Even meat eaters will enjoy this fine substitution for beef bourguignon. Turn the page for the recipe!

Heap on more wood! The wind is chill; But let it whistle as it will, We'll keep our Christmas merry still.
— SIR WALTER SCOTT

Chestnut Bourguignon Pie (Serves 4 to 6)

The day before making this delicious pie, soak the chestnuts in cold water for about 6 to 8 hours, then drain.

¼ pound dried chestnuts
2 bay leaves
1 sprig rosemary
1 cup red wine
1¼ cups vegetable stock
8 shallots, peeled
1 tablespoon butter
¼ pound chestnut mushrooms

¼ pound button mushrooms
2 teaspoons Dijon mustard
2 tablespoons soy sauce
1 tablespoon finely chopped parsley
Salt and freshly ground black pepper, to taste
8 ounces vegetarian puff pastry

1. Place the chestnuts, bay leaves, and rosemary in a saucepan along with the vegetable stock and ½ cup of the red wine. Gently simmer for about an hour, or until the chestnuts are tender. Drain the chestnuts, reserving the liquid.

2. Preheat the oven to 400°F.

3. Fry the shallots in the butter until slightly browned, then add the mushrooms and sauté for 5 minutes. Add the chestnuts, the remaining red wine, and enough of the reserved liquid to cover, and stir in the mustard, soy sauce, and parsley. Bring to a boil and simmer for 30 minutes. Season to taste.

4. Put the mixture in a pie dish. Roll out the pastry on a floured surface, place over the top of the dish and trim around the edges. Bake for 20 minutes or until golden brown.

The Twelve Days of Christmas

A partridge in a pear tree
Two turtle doves
Three French hens
Four calling birds
Five gold rings
Six geese a-laying
Seven swans a-swimming
Eight maids a-milking
Nine ladies dancing
Ten lords a-leaping
Eleven pipers piping
Twelve drummers drumming

All I Want for Christmas . . .

Christmas is a time for peace on Earth and goodwill to all. It is also a time for presents. Whatever you may feel about the commercialization of Christmas, unless you are the modern reincarnation of Ebenezer Scrooge, each year you most probably have to tackle the task of planning and budgeting for the annual exchange of gifts. If you don't put enough thought into the process, it is all too easy to end up in a frenzy of last-minute impulse buying, which inevitably means hugely overspending on an assortment of odds and ends that you are not sure anybody will like. This is not to say that you should rush out and buy all your gifts for the following year in January, though. Just a little advance planning and some creative thinking will ensure your popularity this Christmas.

Planning ahead

Lists

The good old list is your friend; use him well. Keep a notebook in a drawer somewhere so you can jot down gift ideas throughout the year. Next time Auntie Mabel mentions that she's smashed another plate from her precious dinner-service set, make a note of it. Come Christmas or her birthday, you can track down a replacement and voilà! Instant Brownie points for showing that you were listening and cared enough to remember.

Budgets

Settle on a budget that is within your means and stick to it. If you don't keep track of what you are spending, you'll end up crying over your post-Christmas bank statement. Successful gift giving does not mean splurging on expensive designer goods that will inevitably end up stashed away in the back of a closet. It's usually the inexpensive, thoughtful presents that are the most cherished. A new edition of a favorite childhood book is worth ten stainless-steel espresso machines that will never be used. Have a bit of extra cash set aside as a contingency. That way, if you spot the perfect present for that difficult-to-buy-for teenager (who already has every gadget known to man), but it costs a little more than you were planning to spend, you can go ahead and get it without feeling guilty about overspending or having to cut back elsewhere.

Avoiding the Mall

For the shopaholics among us, there's much pleasure to be had in the annual pilgrimage to the mall, with its Christmas lights and window displays. For those who dread the crowds and the lines, there are, thankfully, alternatives.

Catalogs

Most of the major stores produce Christmas catalogs that you can send for or pick up next time you are there. The convenience of being able to shop from home is great, but there are a few things you should watch out for:

❄ Don't be tempted to impulse buy. Have a clear idea in your head of what you are looking for and how much you want to spend before you start flipping through the pages.

❄ Do thoroughly read the payment terms on store cards before you place an order. In particular, always check the interest rates, which are often very high. Always pay off your purchases in full if you can afford it (and you should be able to, if you are sticking to your carefully planned budget).

❄ Do check the terms of delivery to make sure you order your gifts in time and that there will be someone at home to accept the delivery.

❄ Do check the return policy.

The Internet

The great thing about shopping on the Web, apart from the convenience, is that you can buy pretty much anything under the sun, and many things that you won't be able to find in stores. All the dos and don'ts listed above apply to Internet shopping as well, but there are a few other things to consider.

Security is an important issue. Do your homework before you whip out your credit card and thoroughly research the company you want to buy from. There are Web sites that list only secure shopping sites, and which give them a rating based on security, customer service, range of goods, and price. Always read the site's security policy. Many sites offer an alternative telephone payment service. Use this if you are nervous about putting your account details online. Always print out copies of your order details and keep them in a safe place.

Internet auction sites like eBay are incredibly popular and there are fantastic bargains to be had. Bear in mind, though, that in most cases you will be buying from individuals rather than companies and so there is more chance of late delivery (or no delivery) and of goods not being as described. Although these sites offer various means of redress if you are not happy with the service you receive, it will inevitably take time to clear up any problems, so order well ahead of time. Only buy from sellers with a good track record and positive customer feedback. Carefully read the seller's description of the goods before you make a bid and print a copy for your records. Save and print out any e-mails exchanged. Never do deals with sellers outside of the site — some fraudsters will e-mail people who have lost out on an auction with offers of similar goods. If you receive an e-mail like this, do not reply to it — pass it on to the auction site.

December 25, 1868

President Andrew Johnson grants unconditional pardon to everyone involved in the Southern rebellion against the United States.

To re-gift or not to re-gift?

Although some people have re-gifting down to a fine art (see page 13 for an example of truly imaginative re-gifting), the pitfalls are such that it is generally best avoided. The only time it is acceptable is if the gift is a genuinely good one, just not quite to your taste or you already have a similar item. If you think so little of someone that you are happy to give them the hideous Donald Duck socks your Uncle Albert gave you last year, then it's best to forgo a gift altogether and just send a friendly card. If you can't bear to throw your unwanted presents away; donate them to charity. Someone out there might like them, it's just unlikely that it will be the person you're planning on giving them to.

If you must re-gift, always remember the golden rule: Keep track of who gave you what!

Grab bags

If you're hosting or attending a large gathering of family and friends, instead of buying a gift for each and every person, why not suggest a grab-bag exchange? Each person spends a pre-agreed amount on just one gift. All the gifts are wrapped and placed in a large sack, and everyone picks a number out of a hat. "Number one" picks out a gift and opens it in front of everyone else, then "number two" has a turn, and so on. Once everyone has a present, the exchanging begins. Number one has first choice to swap his or her gift with someone else's, then everyone else has a go in order, with the person who picked the final number having the last say.

Christmas Traditions:

THE CHRISTMAS TREE

The Christmas tree tradition most likely has its origins in pagan times, when evergreens were symbolic of new life and hope for the coming year.

The fir tree, however, also has a place in early Christianity. Saint Boniface was born in England in 675 and dedicated his life to converting the pagans. In 719, he was sent to Germany by Pope Gregory II to continue his missionary work. It is said that at Geismar he came across a group of pagans worshipping an oak tree, which was associated with the god Thor, and he cut it down in a fit of anger. In its place sprung a fir tree, and Boniface declared that this was to be the new Christian symbol.

But it was not until much later that the Christmas tree as we know it came to be. A plaque in the town square in

Riga, Latvia, declares that the first "New Year's tree" was to be found there in 1510. At around the same time, it is said that the German theologian Martin Luther was walking in an evergreen forest at night and was so struck by the beauty of the stars shining through the branches that he brought a tree home and decorated it with candles.

The first record of a decorated fir tree associated with Christmas time comes from Bremen, Germany, in 1570, where a fir tree was brought into the guildhall and decorated with fruit and nuts, which were then given to the local children on Christmas Day.

Many people believe that it was Queen Victoria's consort, Prince Albert, who introduced the Christmas tree tradition, already widespread in his native Germany, to Britain. However, records dating from 1800 show that the queen's grandmother, Charlotte, also a German, brought the custom to King George III's court. In 1889, the tradition of having a Christmas tree in the White House began during the presidency of Benjamin Harrison. The tradition has since grown in popularity and has come to reflect the times and tastes of the First Family.

Choosing the Right Christmas Tree

The Christmas tree has had an essential role in Yuletide celebrations for hundreds of years. These days there are so many options available that choosing a tree can be confusing. Whether you prefer the delicious scent of a traditional fir, the convenience of an artificial tree, or want to try something a little bit different, this handy guide will help you make that all-important decision.

Traditional trees

Evergreen conifers are the trees traditionally associated with Christmas and there are many varieties available to choose from. Some of the most popular to be found for sale in the United States are listed here, along with some pros and cons to consider when making your decision.

Norway Spruce: Generally among the cheapest. Has an attractive bushy shape, but the needles are prickly and sparse, and tend to shed earlier than other varieties. Buy it as near to Christmas as possible and keep it well watered.

Noble Fir: Has a lovely deep-green color and a full, bushy shape. There's plenty of space between the branches and the needles are not too prickly, making it easy to decorate.

Douglas Fir: Nationally, one of the most popular Christmas tree species because of its dense, bushy shape and sweet scent. Its needles are dark green or blue-green and soft to the touch.

Blue Spruce: Has beautiful silver-blue foliage and is one of the most aromatic trees. It retains its needles quite well, but they are very sharp, so be careful!

Scotch Pine: Has a very attractive, full shape. Its long, prickly needles can make it tricky to decorate, but it retains them extremely well. Its branches are not very sturdy, so avoid heavy ornaments.

Why does Father Christmas cry a lot?

Because he gets a little santamental.

Caring for your tree

POTTED TREES

Live, potted trees will last much longer than cut trees and are very easy to care for: Just make sure you keep the soil moist at all times, as you would with any other household plant. If you have the outdoor space available, consider planting your tree outside after the Christmas season. If you're planning to do this, here are some things to keep in mind:

❄ Carefully research the type of tree that will suit the space you have available and the environmental conditions in your area.

❄ Don't keep your tree indoors for too long—five to seven days is the maximum—and keep it away from radiators and other sources of heat.

❄ Keep your tree outside in its pot for a month before you plant it so that it can acclimatize.

❄ Dig a hole that is as deep as the measurement from the bottom of the root-ball to the soil level and double the width of the root-ball.

❄ When you are ready to plant, loosen up the outside roots a bit. Keep the soil around the tree weed-free and well watered. When the ground has frozen over, cover it with mulch.

Cut trees

※ Invest in a good stand that can be reused every year. Always fill the stand with water, not soil or sand, and refill it every day.

※ Before you bring your tree indoors, cut about an inch off the trunk—this will help the tree to take up water—and give it a shake to get rid of any loose needles.

※ Keep the tree away from any sources of heat.

※ When Christmas is over, research any tree-recycling services that might be available in your area.

Alternative live trees

Other types of trees that can be grown and kept in pots make for attractive, original, and environmentally friendly alternatives to the traditional tree. Consider bay laurel trees, holly trees, and citrus trees, and tailor your ornamentation accordingly. Bay laurels, for example, look wonderful when decorated with miniature baubles. An indoor lemon tree can be adorned with bows of yellow ribbon, with a matching length of ribbon wound around the trunk.

What did Santa say to Mrs. Claus when he looked out the window?

"Looks like rain, dear."

Artificial trees

Many people turn up their noses at the idea of an artificial tree, but in these environmentally conscious times, they are becoming more and more popular. The trees available nowadays are a far cry from the lurid, plastic creations of the past. You are not limited to imitation firs: How about a beautiful twig tree for a natural look, or a modern, minimalist metal tree? There's something out there to suit every budget, but consider spending a little more to ensure a quality tree. You'll be using it year after year, after all, so you'll be saving money in the end. And be sure to investigate suitable recycling options when you decide that its best Christmases are behind it.

I heard the bells on Christmas Day
Their old familiar carols play,
And wild and sweet
The words repeat
Of peace on earth, goodwill to men!
— HENRY WADSWORTH LONGFELLOW

Thank You Very Much . . .

Dear [name of relative with no taste],

I wish you had been here to witness the gasps of awe when I unwrapped the delightful neon green sweater/novelty fake-fur lampshade/ pink ceramic kitten. Your gift was the cause of much joy and laughter in our household, and for that I thank you.

We were terrified that your precious gift might be inadvertently damaged, so we found it a safe home in a dark corner of a closet, where it will remain forever.

Yours sincerely,

Christmas Around the World

If you think the idea of a fat old man and a bunch of elves delivering presents to all the children in the world in just one night is wacky, you'll be amazed at some of the weird and wonderful ways other countries celebrate the festive season.

Greece

The Greeks don't go for Christmas trees. Instead many homes display a wooden bowl filled with holy water, over which a sprig of basil wrapped around a wooden cross is suspended. Every day throughout the twelve days of Christmas, a household member will dip the cross in the holy water and sprinkle it around the house. This is thought to keep away the *Killantzaroi*, or mischievous goblins who enter homes via the chimney during this time of year and cause mayhem.

Greenland

If you're sick of the same old turkey dinner year after year, why not try the delicious-sounding *kiviak*, the traditional Christmas fare of Greenland? *Kiviak* is raw auk meat that has been wrapped in sealskin and buried for several months, until it is nicely decomposed and suitably smelly. Yummy!

Guatemala

In the weeks before Christmas, Guatemalans believe that the devil runs riot. Guatemalans "celebrate" this by dressing up in suitably demonic style and chasing children through the streets. This culminates in *La Quema del Diablo*, or "The Burning of the Devil," on December 7, when households gather together unwanted items and place them outside where they are set on fire in an attempt to drive the devil away.

Iceland

The children of Iceland have not one but thirteen Santas who enter homes one by one on each of the thirteen days leading up to Christmas. But as it turns out, these *Jolasveinar*, or "Christmas Lads," are actually hideous trolls with names like Meat Hook and Door Slammer.

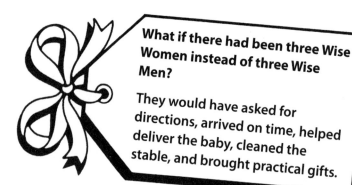

What if there had been three Wise Women instead of three Wise Men?

They would have asked for directions, arrived on time, helped deliver the baby, cleaned the stable, and brought practical gifts.

Mexico

The residents of Oaxaca, Mexico, have a truly unique Christmas celebration: *Noche de Rabanos,* or "Night of the Radishes"—celebrated on December 23, and commemorating the introduction of the radish by Spanish colonists in the mid-nineteenth century. The radishes grown in the region are enormous, measuring up to 2 feet in length and weighing up to 10 pounds, and every year a contest is held to see who can carve them into the most elaborate Nativity figurines or scenes. All hail the mighty radish!

Poland

In Poland, Christmas Eve is traditionally a night when magic abounds. It is said that people gain fortune-telling powers and animals are able to speak in human voices. Many of these old traditions are still practiced in the form of general Christmas fun and games. For example, unmarried girls are blindfolded on the way to Midnight Mass and try to touch a fence picket. If it is smooth and straight, they will find a good husband; if it is crooked, they will attract a less than ideal spouse.

Spain

From the Catalan region of Spain comes what is undoubtedly the strangest of Christmas figures—the *Caganer*, literally translated as "the defecator." The figure is portrayed squatting, with its pants around its ankles—the rest can be left to your imagination. The origins of the *Caganer* are unclear, but is has been around since the seventeenth century and is an essential, if incongruous, part of any Catalonian Nativity scene. In fact, there was a public outcry in 2005, when the Barcelona city council commissioned a Nativity scene that did not include a *Caganer*.

Ukraine

If you're an arachnophobe, you will want to steer clear of the Ukraine at Christmas, because spiders are practically ushered into homes around the country at this time of year. The practice comes from an old folktale about a poor family who were visited by magic spiders one Christmas that turned all the webs in the house into silver and gold.

What do you call someone who doesn't believe in Father Christmas?

A rebel without a Claus.

Venezuela

The people of Caracas have an unusual way of getting to Midnight Mass on Christmas Eve: They rollerskate. The streets of the capital are closed to traffic until the early hours of the morning so that the speed-loving worshippers can make their journey in safety. It is also traditional for the children of Caracas to tie a piece of string to one of their big toes before they go to bed and hang the other end out of the window, so that the rollerskaters can wake them up by tugging on them as they pass.

Wales

Forget Santa. The Welsh have their own jolly festive figure in the shape of a horse's skull on a pole, carried by a person hidden under draped sheets. The *Mari Lwyd* wanders the streets accompanied by a band of singers and anyone who is "bitten" by the skull has to pay a fine. It is also taken from house to house, where the merry group exchanges banter and insults with the homeowners.

Pack Up Your Troubles

If the thought of yet another Christmas of last-minute panicking, endless chores, and catering for ungrateful family members is getting you down, how about taking a trip of a lifetime and letting someone else do all the hard work? Here, for your consideration, are just a few of the top Christmas destinations around the world.

Lapland

Situated mostly in the Arctic Circle, the one thing you are guaranteed in Lapland is snow. Lots of it. At Christmastime it is very cold (temperatures can drop as low as $-40°F$) and constantly dark, but if you're lucky you might catch a glimpse of the magnificent northern lights.

As well as being the home of all things Santa-related, Lapland has plenty of other things to do, among them sled-dog rides, cross-country skiing, or hiking in one of the many national parks. The more adventurous should spend a night or two at the famous Icehotel in Swedish Lapland, where everything, including the beds, is made from ice. Brrr!

Rome

For a traditional Christmas steeped in culture, Rome is the place to go. Visit the impressive Christmas tree and lifesize Nativity scene in Saint Peter's Square, or the city's official *crèche* on the Spanish Steps. The atmospheric Midnight Mass in Saint Peter's Basilica is a must, as is the pope's Christmas Day blessing. The famous Piazza Navona Christmas Market, with its stalls crammed with toys and edible goodies, is a treat for the whole family. In true Italian style, food is all-important at this time of the year. Feast on the traditional Christmas Eve *capitone*—fried eel—and gorge on some of Italy's famous Christmas candy made from honey and almonds.

New York

The holiday season kicks off in November with Macy's world-famous Thanksgiving Day Parade, an annual extravaganza that has taken place since 1924. Rockefeller Center is the place to go for all things Christmassy. There you will find Radio City Music Hall, which annually hosts the Radio City Christmas Spectacular from November to early January that is seen by more than a million people every year. Rockefeller Center is also home to the mother of all Christmas trees, typically more than 65 feet tall and decorated with more than 25,000 lights, and its famous sunken ice-skating rink is one of the most popular Christmas destinations in the city.

Edinburgh

If nonstop partying is what you're after, spend the holidays in Edinburgh. The Winter Festival begins in late November, with the switching on of the city's spectacular Christmas lights, and culminates in four days of Hogmanay revelry. The Winter Wonderland is the highlight of the festival, a heady mix of fairground rides, a huge outdoor skating rink, and a traditional Christmas market. The annual Santa Run is a lot of fun, too, with the city trying to break the record for the largest gathering of Santas running for charity.

Melbourne

If you're dreaming of a white Christmas, then you'll probably want to pass on Christmas Down Under. With temperatures that can soar to a sweltering 100°F, most Australians can be found on the beach roasting themselves rather than a turkey, hoping to catch a glimpse of Santa arriving on a surfboard or water skis. If the idea of relaxing on the beach with a Christmas Day picnic lunch appeals to you, head to Melbourne. On Christmas Eve, tens of thousands of people gather under the stars for the spectacular Carols by Candlelight concert, held at the Sidney Myer Music Bowl.

Christmas Traditions:

CAROLING

The word *carol* comes from the Greek *choraulein*, a dance accompanied by flute music, and the French *caroller*, meaning "to dance around in a circle." Carols are said to have been introduced into church services in the thirteenth century by Saint Francis of Assisi. At first, they were sung at times of general celebration, but later they became associated specifically with the Nativity and were sung at Christmas.

The practice of caroling can be linked to ancient Rome and the Mummers, who were troupes of singers and dancers that went from house to house during the winter festival of Saturnalia. In the Middle Ages, wassailing, which comes from the old English term *waes hael* meaning "be well," was practiced by peasants who visited their feudal lords at the beginning of each year to sing and bless their homes in exchange for wassail, a hot, spiced punch, and other favors. Although caroling today conjures up cozy images of wholesome children singing about the birth of Christ, some of the early songs have rather threatening overtones. Wassailers were often groups of rowdy young men who saw it as their right to gain favors from the wealthy at this time of year, and woe betide anyone who refused them entry:

> "We have come to claim our right
> And if you don't open up your door,
> We'll lay you flat upon the floor."

Christmas gift suggestions:
To your enemy, forgiveness.
To an opponent, tolerance.
To a friend, your heart.
To a customer, service.
To all, charity.
To every child, a good example.
To yourself, respect.

— OREN ARNOLD

Tree Decorations

Although you can buy ornaments in every shape and color under the sun, why not make a few of your own? It will add a personal touch to your tree and is a fun activity for the whole family. Here are just a couple of ideas to get the ball rolling.

Orange clove pomanders

Not only are these traditional pomanders attractive ornaments, but they also fill the house with a delicious, Christmassy fragrance. The spice mix adds even more scent, but you can leave it out if you prefer.

1. Wash some fresh oranges and pat them dry.

2. In a bowl, mix together equal amounts of ground cinnamon, ground nutmeg, allspice, ground cloves, and orrisroot powder. The orrisroot acts as a preservative, making for a longer-lasting fragrance.

3. Stud the fruit with whole cloves, leaving about ¼ inch between each one. You can cover the whole orange evenly with cloves, or be a little more artistic and make a pattern.

4. Roll the studded oranges in the spice mix and leave them in a warm place to dry. It can take up to a month for them to dry out properly, so plan ahead!

5. Once they are dry, tie ribbons around them or hook ornament hangers through the tops of the oranges and hang them on the tree.

Dough ornaments

Kids will love to help make these, and you can produce any shape you can think of, from angels to stars to reindeer. One batch of dough makes several ornaments. They're not edible, though, so don't be tempted to nibble them!

1. In a bowl, mix together 4 cups of flour and 2 cups of salt. Slowly add 2 cups cold water, mixing all the time, until you have a smooth dough. Roll out the dough on a floured surface until it is about ¼ inch thick.

2. Draw the shapes you desire onto a piece of thick cardboard and cut them out. Place the templates on the dough and cut around them with a sharp knife. Make a hole at the top of each shape with a toothpick (ensuring the hole is big enough to thread string through) and place them on an ungreased baking tray. Bake in a 250°F oven for two hours or until the dough is hard but not brown.

3. Once the shapes have cooled, use acrylic paints to decorate them. Thread some decorative string through the holes you've made and hang them on the tree.

Wreath making

For many people, wreaths are an integral part of Christmastime decoration. Traditionally, they were a symbol of hope for the coming of spring, with the evergreen foliage and the circular shape representing life during the dead of winter. You can hang your homemade wreaths on your door or walls, or use one as a decorative centerpiece for your table, with a candle placed in the middle.

It is possible to buy inexpensive wreath frames from florists, garden centers, or craft shops, but it is easy to make your own by simply bending a wire coat hanger into a circular shape.

To create a traditional wreath, gather various lengths of evergreen foliage and arrange them around the frame, using thin wire to secure them. Additional decorations can be attached with more wire or glue and can include all sorts of things: dried berries, pinecones, nuts (either in their natural state or spray-painted silver or gold), lengths of colored ribbon, dried orange slices, cinnamon sticks, baubles, dried flowers, and so on.

Reindeer Facts

They may not be able to fly through the air and land gracefully and noiselessly on rooftops as festive legend would have it, but reindeer are surprising animals, nonetheless.

❄ Both male and female reindeer have antlers, the only species of deer to display this trait. Every reindeer grows a new set annually.

❄ Unless they are neutered, male reindeer shed their antlers at the beginning of winter and females shed theirs in spring. Therefore, all Santa's reindeer must either be female or neutered males.

❄ Rudolph of red-nosed fame was originally going to be named either Rollo or Reginald, until creator Robert May's four-year-old daughter Barbara expressed a preference for Rudolph.

✳ Reindeer have been around for a long time. Ice Age engravings in a cave in France depict what is thought to be reindeer, and the artwork has been dated from 12,000 to 10,500 B.C.

✳ Reindeer don't sink into the snow despite their size because their weight is distributed over a large area due to their wide, splayed hooves.

✳ Reindeer are herbivores, feeding on grasses, mosses, leaves, and lichens.

✳ A reindeer can pull twice its body weight for up to 40 miles.

December 25,
1939
Department store
Montgomery Ward
introduces Rudolph the
Red-Nosed Reindeer to
the world.

True Christmas Stories: "Yes, Virginia"

In 1897, eight-year-old Virginia O'Hanlon wrote the following letter to Francis P. Church, the editor of the *New York Sun*.

Dear Editor

I am 8 years old. Some of my little friends say there is no Santa Claus. Papa says, "If you see it in the Sun, it's so." Please tell me the truth, is there a Santa Claus?

Virginia O'Hanlon

The editor's reply became instantly famous and more than one hundred years later it continues to be the most reprinted editorial ever to run in an English-language newspaper.

Virginia, your little friends are wrong. They have been affected by the skepticism of a skeptical age. They do not believe except they see. They think that nothing can be which is not comprehensible by their little minds. All minds, Virginia, whether they be men's or children's, are little. In this great universe of ours, man is a mere insect, an ant, in his intellect as compared with the boundless world about him, as measured by the intelligence capable of grasping the whole of truth and knowledge.

Yes, Virginia, there is a Santa Claus. He exists as certainly as love and generosity and devotion exist, and you know that they abound and give to your life its highest beauty and joy. Alas! How dreary would be the world if there were no Santa Claus! It would be as dreary as if there were no Virginias. There would be no childlike faith then, no poetry, no romance to make tolerable this existence. We should have no enjoyment, except in sense and sight. The external light with which childhood fills the world would be extinguished.

Not believe in Santa Claus! You might as well not believe in fairies. You might get your papa to hire men to watch in all the chimneys on Christmas Eve to catch Santa Claus, but even if you did not see Santa Claus coming down, what would that prove? Nobody sees Santa Claus, but that is no sign that there is no Santa Claus. The most real things in the world are those that neither children nor men can see. Did you ever see fairies dancing on the lawn?

Of course not, but that's no proof that they are not there. Nobody can conceive or imagine all the wonders there are unseen and unseeable in the world. You tear apart the baby's rattle and see what makes the noise inside, but there is a veil covering the unseen world that not the strongest man, nor even the united strength of all the strongest men who ever lived could tear apart. Only faith, poetry, love, romance, can push aside that curtain and view and picture the supernal beauty and glory beyond.

Is it all real? Ah, Virginia, in all this world there is nothing else real and abiding.

No Santa Claus? Thank God, he lives and lives forever. A thousand years from now, Virginia, nay 10 times 10,000 years from now, he will continue to make glad the heart of childhood.

Merry Christmas and a Happy New Year!!!!

It was always said of him, that he knew how to keep Christmas well, if any man alive possessed the knowledge. May that be truly said of us, and all of us! And so, as Tiny Tim observed, "God Bless Us, Every One!"

— Charles Dickens

Christmas Practical Jokes

Goodwill to men is all well and good, but getting a chuckle at someone else's expense is always fun, and Christmas is about enjoying yourself, after all. Just pick your victims wisely and don't expect much in the way of presents from them this year.

❄ Sick of those coworkers who always jet off on an expensive Caribbean holiday just before Christmas to work on their tans for the party season? While they're away, painstakingly gift-wrap everything on and in, their desks: computer monitor, mouse, individual pens, stapler, phone . . . you get the picture. And use tacky wrapping paper, with lots of tape.

❄ Make the biggest snowball you possibly can—we're talking *huge* here. Get a friend or two to help out. When it's done, haul it up to your victim's bedroom and place it in the middle of his or her bed. Turn off the heat and open the window so that it doesn't melt too fast. Refuse to help as your victim frantically tries to get rid of it before his or her sheets get totally soaked.

❄ If you've received one of those annoying Christmas cards that play a jingle every time you open it, take it apart and remove the music chip. Attach it to the hinge of a door (a closet door works well) so that it activates whenever the door is opened. Your victim won't be able to figure out where it is coming from, and those chips keep going for a long time.

❄ This is a lot of fun if you're feeling a little mischievous during a family Christmas party. Choose your "victim," sit him or her in a chair, and explain that you'd like him or her to take part in a blindfolded coordination test — a test, incidentally, that only the very brightest succeed at. Sit in front of the victim and hold up your hands, palms facing, about a ruler's width apart. Now, ask your victim to place his or her hands together and pass them between your hands and back out again, without touching your hands in the process. This counts as "1," you inform your victim, and the smartest people can do this forty or fifty times. Now that your victim has practiced, remind him or her that the test must be conducted blindfolded. Once this is done, resume the position of your hands, ask your victim to start, counting as he or she does so. After thirty seconds or so, walk quietly away and watch your victim rock his or her hands back and forth, counting aloud like someone possessed. Try not to laugh and encourage others to come and have a look!

❄ When the temperature plummets, sneak out late one night and fill your victim's outdoor trash cans with water, which will quickly become a couple of hundred pounds of solid ice.

❄ When it's time for the annual nightmare that is the office "Secret Santa," replace all the slips of paper with your coworkers' names on them with slips on which only your own name appears. Reap the rewards and then look for a new job.

❄ Take two sticky notes and write "Merry Christmas!" on them. Place these notes on the glass of the office photocopier, put the lid down, and press the COPY button. Move the notes and repeat. Do this several times. When the copies emerge with the festive message printed on them, take these sheets and put them back into the paper trays. Now, watch as the unsuspecting victim uses the photocopier, picks up his or her copies . . . and sees the mysterious notes on the documents. Have a chuckle to yourself when he or she opens the lid and searches in vain for the source of the spooky Yuletide messages that are mysteriously appearing!

❄ Dress up like the Easter Bunny and pick a fight with a department-store Santa, telling him, "This town ain't big enough for the both of us."

❄ Liven up a dull Christmas party by addressing all the men as "Mrs." and the women as "Mr."

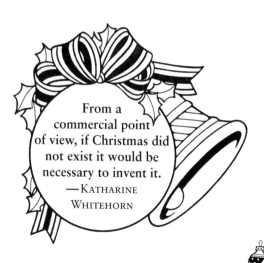

From a commercial point of view, if Christmas did not exist it would be necessary to invent it.
—KATHARINE WHITEHORN

69

How to Host a Christmas Party: Part Two

Our guide to throwing the best party in town continues.

How to be a good host

Being a good host means making sure that things run smoothly and that your guests are adequately fed and watered and are mingling happily, rather than standing around awkwardly staring at the floor. It doesn't mean rushing around like a headless chicken, fretting about every little thing, and panicking when something goes wrong. If you are uptight, your guests will be, too. If you feel yourself getting anxious, take a deep breath and relax. It's your party; you should enjoy it, too! If you're hosting the party on your own, rope in a couple of friends to help out with handing out snacks and keeping glasses full.

Make an effort to greet each and every guest as he or she arrives. This doesn't mean you have to hover by the front door all night waiting for

70

stragglers. Just be alert and listen for the doorbell. Immediately offer a drink, listing what is available. If you just say, "What would you like to drink?" most people will reply, "Oh, whatever you've got open," and might then be stuck with a drink they don't like.

If your guests don't all know one another, make the necessary introductions. Always be on the lookout for people who are standing alone. If you spot someone who is alone, lead him or her over to a group and introduce a topic of conversation to which you know he or she will be able to contribute.

Food

You'll need to provide plenty of food to make sure your guests are not hungry. Finger food is by far the best option because your guests won't have to line up while performing complicated balancing acts with plates, knives, forks, and glasses. Just make sure you provide plenty of napkins and keep the food circulating throughout the evening.

You should allow about ten canapés or snacks per person—you'll probably have leftovers, but it's better to have too much food than not enough. Buy some cheap disposable containers so that you can offer leftovers to guests as they leave if you have a lot of surplus food.

Serve a good variety of snacks and plenty of vegetarian options.

All supermarkets stock pre-made party platters, so there's absolutely no need to cook everything yourself, but if you do want to impress your guests with your culinary skills, choose food that can be prepared in advance and served cold or heated up at the last minute. Below are a few suggestions for unique snacks.

Cranberry Phyllo Rolls (Makes 15 to 20 rolls)

½ cup dried cranberries
½ cup ground almonds
1 tablespoon capers in vinegar, drained

1 tablespoon chopped fresh dill
¼ teaspoon cumin
3 (12 x 17 inch) sheets phyllo
1 tablespoon butter, melted

1. Preheat the oven to 400°F.

2. Put the dried cranberries in a bowl, cover them with boiling water, and leave them to soak for about 20 minutes. When they are soft, drain them and put them in a food processor along with the ground almonds, capers, dill, and cumin. Blend until you have a purée.

3. Lay out a sheet of phyllo and brush it with the melted butter. Spoon a strip of the cranberry mixture along the bottom of the sheet, about an inch above the edge. Fold the bottom edge over the filling and then continue to roll until you have a tight tube. Cut off the two ends and then cut into 2-inch pieces. Repeat this with the

other sheets of phyllo, then place them on a baking tray and bake for 15 to 20 minutes, until golden. Can be served straight from the oven or cold.

Bruschetta with Peppers and Pesto
(Makes 15 to 20 pieces)

For the bruschetta
2 baguettes
3 garlic cloves, peeled
Olive oil, for drizzling

For the peppers
6 red peppers
6 garlic cloves, finely chopped
5 shallots, finely chopped
Juice of 2 lemons
1 teaspoon dried oregano
½ cup olive oil
3 tablespoons sherry vinegar
Salt
Freshly ground black pepper
1 (4-ounce) jar pesto

1. Preheat the oven to 400° F.

2. Cut the bread into slices about half an inch thick. Rub one side of each slice all over with the whole garlic cloves and drizzle with olive oil. Place on a baking tray and bake for 2 to 3 minutes, until they are golden brown. Remove from the oven and leave to cool.

3. Put the whole peppers on a baking tray and bake them for about 30 minutes, or until they are blackened. Remove them from the oven and immediately put them into a paper bag, seal it, and leave to cool.

Once cool, it should be easy to peel off the skins. Cut the peppers into long strips, discarding the core and seeds.

4. In a bowl, mix together the garlic, shallots, lemon juice, oregano, olive oil, and sherry vinegar. Season to taste, add the peppers, toss everything together and set aside for a couple of hours.

5. When you are ready to serve, simply top each bruschetta with some peppers and a dollop of pesto.

Prosciutto Fig Rolls (Makes 25 pieces)

> 1 pound sliced prosciutto ham
> 1 cup dried figs
> 4 ounces mild, soft goat cheese
> 1 package toothpicks

Cut each slice of prosciutto into three strips. Slice each fig in half, spread with a small dollop of goat cheese, and roll in the strips of prosciutto. Use a toothpick to hold each roll together. This will also make your snacks easy to serve and eat.

Christmas Traditions:

THE YULE LOG

The origins of the yule log can be traced back to the Norsemen of northern Europe. *Jol* or *Jule* (pronounced "Yule") was a festival celebrated on the Winter Solstice in honor of Jolnir, also known as Odin, the god of ecstasy and death. Feasting and drinking would take place around bonfires, and fires would be lit in hearths.

This tradition spread to other parts of Europe, where tree worship was already part of pagan rituals. Households would venture into the woods on Christmas Eve and cut a log from an oak tree, which was then transported home, with much singing and merrymaking along the way. The log would be put on the fire, which would be kept burning for twelve days. This was believed to bring health and productivity to the family and their crops for the coming year and protect them from witchcraft and demons. When the fire was finally extinguished, a small piece of the wood would be kept and used to light the next year's log. Often the ashes would be scattered over the fields to ensure fertility.

Later on, the yule log was used as a decorative centerpiece for the Christmas table, and as stoves replaced giant household hearths, the pastry or chocolate logs we are familiar with today came into being.

Thank You Very Much . . .

Dear [name of arts-and-crafts-obsessed relative],

Every year I await your homemade gift with a sense of breathless anticipation. This Christmas, as always, I was not disappointed. The sweater is superb. Who would have thought that neon pink, brown, and orange would make for such a successful color combination? How clever of you to knit it several sizes too big! You just never know when you might be hit by one of those midlife growth spurts. I will wear it with pride in the privacy of my own home.

Yours sincerely,

Fun and Games

Whether you want to break the ice at a party or simply keep the kids entertained and away from the TV, it's always good to have a few fun games and group activities up your sleeve at Christmas.

For the kids

❄ Ask each child to gather a selection of small household items and wrap them in leftover scraps of wrapping paper. The children then swap their items and get a point for each item they correctly identify without unwrapping it.

❄ Write down a list of anagrams of Christmas words on a sheet of paper and get the children to unscramble as many as they can within a certain time limit, with a prize going to the one who gets the most right.

❄ Pin a white sheet of paper to the wall and place a chair facing it. Position a table behind the chair with a lit lamp on it, shining toward the wall. Each child takes turns sitting in the chair, while the others walk between the lamp and chair one by one. The child who is seated must guess who walked across by his or her shadow.

❄ Place a chair in the middle of the room with a set of keys underneath it. One child is blindfolded and sits in the chair. The others must take turns sneaking up to the chair, stealing the keys, and returning to the starting line without making any noise. If the blindfolded child hears anything, the person attempting the theft is out of the game. The child who gets the farthest is the winner and takes his or her turn in the chair.

❄ Get two children to mime a scene—driving a car, playing tennis, or rowing a boat, for example. At some point shout "Stop!" and the actors must freeze. Another child then takes the place of one of the actors and must adopt the exact same position. Then both children must improvise a different scene according to the positions they are in.

❄ Put an assortment of adult-size clothes into separate bags. Give one bag to each child. Each child must put on every item in the bag over his or her own clothes. The winner is the one who dresses the fastest.

❄ Tear out pages from a magazine that display a complete image on them. Cut each page into smaller pieces to form a jigsaw puzzle. Place each puzzle in a bag or box and hand one to each team. The winning team is the one who completes their puzzle first.

❄ Blow up one balloon per child and write his or her name on it. Hand out a balloon and a sheet of paper to each child. The object of the game is to keep the balloon in the air for as long as possible, using only the paper to waft it.

❄ Organize an indoor treasure hunt. Prepare a goodie bag containing candy or small stocking-stuffer gifts for each child. Hide each bag in a separate location, along with a clue to lead the children to the next goodie bag. Start them off on their group hunt by handing them a written clue to where they can find the first bag.

❄ Each participant chooses the name of a local railroad station and makes this known to the other players. Everyone sits down in a circle except one person who stands in the middle. The person in the middle then says, for example, "This Christmas I went from State Street to Main Street." The two people who are called State and Main Street then must exchange places as fast as possible, while the person in the middle attempts to take over one of the empty places. Every so often, the person in the middle can shout "all change," upon which everyone must get up and swap places, and the player left without a seat must stay in the middle.

❄ Divide everyone into two teams. Attach two spoons to very long pieces of string and give one to each team. The two teams then line up facing each other and on the word *go* they must link themselves together by passing their spoon along the line. The spoon must be passed down the clothes of one team member and then up the clothes of the next team member. The quickest team wins.

❄ Each player (or victim!) takes turns being blindfolded. Another player holds his or her nose while feeding the victim either a slice of cooked brussels sprout or a piece of chocolate truffle. The victim has to guess what he or she is actually eating. Guessing is harder than it seems, because it's difficult to taste anything when your nose is being held!

For the adults

❄ Each guest takes a turn standing, and makes three statements about him or herself, one of which must be a lie. Everyone must then guess which statement is the lie.

❄ Provide each guest with five small pieces of paper and a pencil and ask each one to write down the names of five famous people. Fold the pieces of paper and place them in a hat or box. Divide everyone into groups of two and ask one person to pick a piece of paper. That person must provide clues about the celebrity's identity until his or her partner gets it right, without mentioning the person's name. Each couple has thirty seconds to guess as many as they can, and a point is awarded for every correct answer.

❄ Another variation of the "name game" involves asking everyone to write down the name of a famous person on a piece of paper. Jumble up the names and hand one out to each guest. Get people mingling and chatting, but each guest must act in character while others try to guess who he or she is supposed to be.

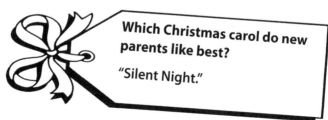

Which Christmas carol do new parents like best?

"Silent Night."

❄ Choose four people to start off this game. Three of the four leave the room and the fourth is asked by the host to mime out a scene. It should be something unusual and difficult to act out, such as trying to break into a locked car or stepping into a bathtub full of pudding. One of the group is then called back in and watches the mime. The original actor then sits back down, and the second of the group then has to mime what he or she thinks was just performed to the next person in the group, and so it continues. After watching the third mime attempt, the final person in the group has to guess what the scene is all about.

❄ Each player is given a piece of paper with columns headed with categories such as girl's name, boy's name, country, city, river, tree, animal, book, film, etc. One person then randomly chooses a letter of the alphabet, and every participant must write down one thing that begins with that letter for each section. The game stops when one person has finished—it's a race against everyone else. Players are awarded one point if someone else also has the same answer and two points for a unique answer.

❄ All players must sit in a circle. The first participant chooses an adverb—such as humorously, happily, excitedly, mournfully, and so on—and whispers it to the player sitting to his or her right. This player then has to sing a Christmas carol in the manner of the chosen word until the other players have guessed the adverb.

Gift Wrapping Made Easy: Part Two

In Part Two of our guide to gift wrapping, we look at some decorative touches that can make all the difference.

Beautiful bows

Bows are a particularly attractive addition to any package. Most of the gift-wrapping ribbon (i.e., nonfabric ribbon) on sale is curling ribbon and can be used to make these pretty decorations. To curl a strand of ribbon, open up a pair of scissors and run the blunt edge along the entire length of the ribbon in the direction of the ribbon's natural curl. This looks very attractive when applied to the ribbon used to secure the tube in the method detailed on page 17 and 18. In addition, follow the steps below to add a curling ribbon bow to a wrapped box.

1. Cut several long strands of thin ribbon; the more ribbon you use, the more extravagant your bow. Using different colors and textures can work well. Hold them together and use them as if they were one strand.

2. Make sure the box is laid in front of you right side up and place the ribbon over the top.

3. Turn the box over, so that the ribbon is now under the box, and bring the two ends up to the middle. Twist them around each other, then go around the box in the other direction, flipping it over so that it is right side up again.

4. Secure the ends with a tight double knot, then tie the ribbon into a large bow.

5. Cut through the middle of each of the bow's loops and curl each strand as detailed above.

Alternatively, you can use a thicker ribbon to produce a more unusual bow that goes around each corner of the box, rather than the middle.

1. Cut a long length of flat, wide ribbon.

2. Place your wrapped box right side up in front of you and place the ribbon diagonally over the top left corner of the box, making sure you leave a long tail.

3. Hold the ribbon in place, take it around the back of the box, and then back over the front of the bottom right corner.

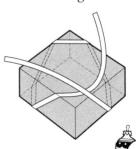

4. Take the ribbon around the back of the bottom left corner and then back over the front to where you started.

5. Secure the ends together by tying a tight double knot, then tie into a bow.

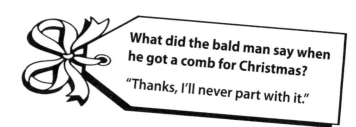

What did the bald man say when he got a comb for Christmas?

"Thanks, I'll never part with it."

Fabric gift bags

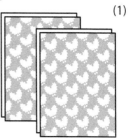
(1)

As an alternative to paper gift wrap, try making a few quick and easy fabric gift bags. All you need are some scraps of colorful material and some plain cotton for the lining (old bedsheets work well).

(1) Cut two pieces of fabric and two pieces of the lining material to size.

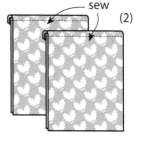
sew (2)

(2) Put one piece of fabric over each piece of lining, fold over the top edges, and sew a hem. This will form the top of the gift bag.

(3) Put the pieces of material together so that the lining is facing the outside, and sew the three unhemmed sides together.

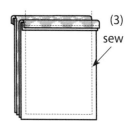
(3)
sew

(4) Turn the bag inside out. Attach a ribbon a couple of inches down from the top of the bag by sewing a few stitches in the middle of the ribbon, at the back of the bag.

(4)

Creative wrapping ideas

If you're feeling adventurous, get creative and try something a little bit different. Here are just a few suggestions:

❄ Join leftover scraps of wrapping paper in contrasting colors and textures and reuse. You can disguise any messy joints with ribbons.

❄ Experiment with other types of paper. Newspaper, for example, may seem like a cheap option, but it looks fantastic when teamed up with a luxurious fabric-ribbon bow in a bright color, and it's a great way to recycle. Pages from the Sunday comics are perfect for wrapping children's presents. Plain brown paper works well when tied up with a length of white gauze or a natural material such as raffia.

❄ Make your own personalized wrapping paper by typing out an appropriate dictionary definition on a piece of blank paper (e.g., "Santa Claus, *n.*, the legendary patron saint of children") and using a photocopier to enlarge it, or by assembling and printing out a collage of family photographs.

❄ Match gifts with appropriate containers. For example, gardening gloves can be presented in a terra-cotta pot, or kitchen implements in a colorful oven mitt.

✳ Make attractive gift boxes for small items out of egg cartons. Cut two sections out and tape or glue them together on one side to form a hinge. Decorate them with paint, glitter, stickers, or anything else you can think of. Fill with tissue paper and pop in the small gift.

✳ There are a multitude of things you can use to embellish your package. Dried or silk flowers, pieces of holly or mistletoe, miniature pinecones, and dried leaves are great for a natural look. Add a feminine touch by wrapping a bead necklace around the gift instead of ribbon. Striped candy canes are colorful adornments that can be enjoyed in other ways once Christmas dinner has been digested. The only limit is your imagination!

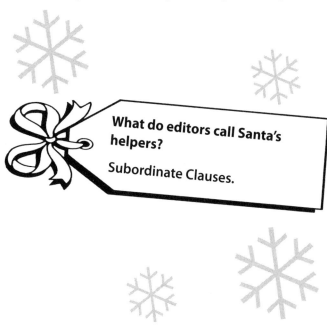

What do editors call Santa's helpers?

Subordinate Clauses.

Christmas Place Names

If the idea of an all-year-round Christmas appeals, consider moving to one of the many festively named spots around the United States, where the celebration will never be far from your mind.

Bethlehem	Pennsylvania
Blitzen	Oregon
Chestnut	Alabama
Christmas City	Utah
Christmas Cove	Maine
Cranberry	West Virginia
Eggnog	Utah
Elf	North Carolina
Holiday Hills	Illinois
Holly	Colorado
Humbug	Arizona
Jolly	Texas
Merry Christmas Creek	Alaska
Mistletoe	Kentucky
Noel	Louisiana
North Pole	Alaska
Partridge	Kansas
Rudolph	Wisconsin
Santa Claus	Indiana
Snow	Oklahoma
Tannenbaum	Arkansas

Gift Ideas

It can be a struggle to think of original and appropriate gifts each year. Give plenty of thought to the person you are buying for. What are her hobbies? Does he have any passions? If in doubt, consult someone who knows the person better than you do. Try to think outside the box and avoid anonymous gifts like toiletries and scented candles. If you're still stuck, check out the following tips for some inspiration.

Children

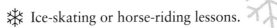

※ Avoid anything to do with the latest crazes. They'll be over before the toy is even out of the box.

※ Always check the manufacturer's age guidelines before buying a toy.

※ Avoid very noisy or disruptive toys if you want to remain friendly with the child's parents.

※ Never buy a child a pet without first consulting the parents.

CONSIDER

※ Ice-skating or horse-riding lessons.

※ Membership to a local zoo. Many zoos offer animal adoption programs. Kids will love visiting their adopted animal and receiving photos and updates.

※ Classic board games.

※ A nicely bound set of classic children's books.

※ A chemistry set or magic kit.

※ A piggy bank with some money in it to start the child off.

※ Personalized stationery.

※ A subscription to a favorite magazine.

Teenagers

❄ Avoid any fashion-related gifts unless it's something they specifically pointed out and asked for. Chances are you'll get it wrong!

❄ Check with the parents as to what is and isn't allowed in the household before you buy anything that could be controversial.

CONSIDER

❄ Gift certificates from a favorite clothing or music store.

❄ Vouchers to download music.

❄ A diary or scrapbook.

❄ Sports equipment.

❄ College fund or savings-account contributions.

❄ Tickets to a concert.

❄ Movie vouchers.

Friends and Family

❄ Avoid appliances like the plague! As a general rule, if it's got a plug, don't buy it.

❄ As with teenagers, it's best to avoid clothes or jewelry unless you are very sure of the person's tastes.

CONSIDER

❄ Activity-related gifts. Web sites offer an enormous variety of prepaid activities, from racecar driving lessons to spa days to cooking courses.

❄ A donation to a favorite charity.

❄ Theater tickets.

❄ Newspaper or magazine subscriptions.

❄ Museum memberships.

❄ Travel vouchers.

❄ A newspaper front page from the day the person was born.

❄ A photo album you've put together of favorite family snapshots.

❄ Tickets to sporting events.

❄ Memorabilia such as sports programs, autographs, or film posters. Check Internet auction sites for these.

Colleagues and Neighbors

❅ Don't overdo it on gifts for people you don't know very well. It will make them feel awkward, particularly if they haven't gotten you anything.

CONSIDER

❅ Homemade edible gifts. Try something a little bit different, rather than the usual batch of chocolate chip cookies. See pages 94 and 95 for inspiration.

❅ Christmas tree ornaments.

❅ A bulb planted in an attractive container that will flower in time for Christmas.

Mankind is a great, an immense family. . . . This is proved by what we feel in our hearts at Christmas.
—POPE JOHN XXIII

Edible Gifts

Unless the recipient is on a severely restricted diet, edible gifts are great at Christmas time. These snacks are delicious and simple to make.

Chocolate Truffles (makes 40–45 truffles)

> 8 ounces good dark chocolate
> 1 cup heavy cream
> Cocoa powder for dusting

1. Break the chocolate into chunks and place in a bowl over a pan of simmering water. Slowly melt the chocolate, stirring constantly.

2. Gently heat the cream in a saucepan until it is warm. Pour the heavy cream over the chocolate, stir in well, and leave to cool and set.

3. Once set, take teaspoons of the mixture, roll into balls, and dust with cocoa powder.

Shortbread (makes 20–24 cookies)

½ cup confectioners' sugar
1 cup butter
Pinch of salt

2 cups flour
Granulated sugar, for sprinkling

1. Beat the sugar and butter until the mixture is creamy and fluffy. In a separate bowl, mix together the salt and flour, then thoroughly combine with the butter mixture.

2. Form the mixture into a ball, then roll it by hand into a tube that is about 2 to 3 inches in diameter. Wrap the tube in plastic wrap and leave it in the fridge until it is hard.

3. Preheat the oven to 325° F. Unwrap the tube and cut into half-inch-thick slices. Sprinkle with granulated sugar and bake for about 20 minutes, until the shortbread is very slightly golden. Cool on a wire rack.

Christmas Traditions:

MISTLETOE

Like so many Christmas traditions that have survived through the ages, the hanging of mistletoe has its origins in pre-Christian times. The Celtic Druids and the ancient Greeks revered the plant, believing it had many mystical and healing properties. To them, its evergreen nature made it a symbol of prosperity and fertility, especially important in the bleak, hard winter months. The practice of hanging mistletoe indoors began in the Middle Ages, when branches were hung over doorways to ward off evil spirits.

The origins of the traditional kiss under the mistletoe are less clear. The mistletoe plant was associated with many ancient Greek fertility and marriage rites. To the Romans, mistletoe was a symbol of peace, and in Norse legend the plant was associated with the goddess of love, Frigga or Freya. The modern practice began in eighteenth-century England. Young women who stood underneath the hanging mistletoe could not refuse a kiss, and if any unfortunate girl should remain unkissed, it was said that she would not marry within the next year.

Leftover Turkey

It happens every year. You buy the biggest turkey you can find for Christmas dinner and are then faced with days of endless turkey sandwiches. These quick and easy recipes offer some creative alternatives for using up your leftover Christmas dinner.

Turkey Enchiladas (Serves 4)

1 cup white and dark cooked turkey meat, shredded	¼ cup chiles, chopped
	8 flour tortillas
1 cup cheddar cheese, grated	1 (14½-ounce) can diced tomatoes

A delicious alternative to turkey sandwiches. If you like a bit of heat, add some small, fiery red chiles; for a sweeter, milder flavor, go with the larger green ones.

1. Preheat the oven to 400°F.

2. Mix together the turkey, cheese, and chiles in a bowl.

3. Spoon some of the turkey mixture on each tortilla. Roll up. Place seam side down in greased baking dish. Cover with tomatoes.

4. Bake for about 25 minutes.

Turkey Chow Mein (Serves 4)

½ cup turkey or chicken stock
1 tablespoon oyster sauce
1 tablespoon soy sauce
1 tablespoon cornstarch
Salt
Freshly ground black pepper
4 tablespoons oil, for stir-frying
1 pound button mushrooms, halved
1 stalk celery, roughly chopped

1 red pepper, roughly chopped
1 red onion, finely chopped
1 clove garlic, finely chopped
2 cups white and dark cooked
    turkey meat, roughly shredded
2 carrots, roughly chopped
1 cup bean sprouts
1 (6-ounce) package crispy chow
    mein noodles

Despite the long list of ingredients, this is a quick, easy, and healthy dish to prepare.

1. To make the sauce, combine the stock, oyster sauce, and soy sauce and whisk in the cornstarch. Season to taste.

2. Heat a wok or frying pan over high heat. Add some of the oil and fry the mushrooms, then remove them from the pan and set aside. Add more oil to the pan and fry the celery and pepper. Remove them from the pan and mix with the mushrooms. Fry the onion and garlic in more oil. Add the turkey and fry for a minute or two, then return the mushrooms and other cooked vegetables to the pan along with the carrots and bean sprouts. Pour the sauce over the mixture and heat until it reaches the boiling point. Turn off the heat, add the noodles, and mix everything together thoroughly. Serve immediately.

Thank You Very Much . . .

Dear [name of relative with a wacky sense of humor],

Thank you so much for the Darth Vader mask/set of plastic comedy pecs/"I'm with stupid" T-shirt. It is hilarious! I laughed so hard, in fact, that I had to be hospitalized following a burst blood vessel. You truly are one of the great wits of our time. We would love to invite you for Christmas next year so that you could entertain us with your amusing anecdotes and uncanny impersonations, but unfortunately we are emigrating to Canada.

Yours sincerely,

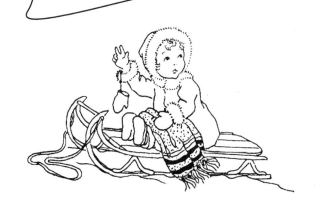

Let It Snow

A miracle has occurred and you've finally gotten the white Christmas you've been dreaming of, so put on a warm coat, get outside, and have some fun! Here are some great suggestions for snowy activities:

❄ Play a game of snow tag. One person is "It" and has to chase and catch the others, but he or she must only tread in the footprints made by those being chased. The first person to be caught is then "It."

❄ Build an outdoor snow lantern. Wait until dusk, then flatten the snow in the area where you want to build your lantern and start making some tightly packed snowballs. Place the snowballs close together to form a circle on the ground, leaving a gap the width of one snowball. Now build a slightly smaller circle of snowballs on top of the first one, this time making the circle complete. Keep building up the lantern until it is the height you want, then top with a single snowball. Light a tea candle and push it through the gap in the first circle, so that it is in the middle of the lantern.

❄ Organize an epic snowball fight. Divide everyone into two teams and have each team build a snow fort—a low wall behind which players can shelter—facing each other but some distance away. A good tip to strengthen your fort is to pour cold water over it so that it ices over, but be careful not to spill any on the ground behind the

wall, otherwise you will find it difficult to stand up! Next, set to work building up an arsenal of snowballs and store them behind your fort. Start the fight! The idea is to "conquer" the enemy fort. Once a player has been hit by a snowball he or she is out and must retire from the game. If all players on a team are out, the opposing team claims the fort as their own.

❄ Create some snow art. Fill spray bottles with water and different food colorings. Flatten an area of snow and get creative.

Christmas Traditions:

HOLLY
AND IVY

Like mistletoe, holly and ivy were important to the ancient Europeans. The fact that they are evergreen plants meant that they were thought of as magical, representing eternal life and the cycle of nature and giving hope for the coming of spring. They were used together in rites because they were said to represent the masculine (holly) and feminine (ivy) elements of nature. This then led to both holly and ivy being introduced into the home to create harmony and balance.

Holly is also associated with the Roman winter festival of Saturnalia, in honor of the god Saturn, which was celebrated much as we celebrate Christmas today, with merrymaking and homes decorated with evergreen plants.

The early Christians associated holly with Christ, with the sharp-edged leaves representing his crown of thorns and the red berries his shed blood.

Christmas Superstitions and Customs

The festive season has inspired a number of rituals and customs—here are just a few.

The Yule Log: Tradition dictates that the Yule Log must not be purchased but must be procured from either your own grounds or neighboring woods. In order to bring good luck to the household, it must be lit with wood from last year's log, and kept burning from Christmas Eve into Christmas Day.

Letting Christmas In: The door of any dwelling should be thrown open at midnight on Christmas Eve to release any trapped evil spirits, then shut. The first member of the household to wake up on Christmas morning may open the door to welcome Christmas in.

Carolers: It is considered very unlucky to allow carolers to leave without offering a "reward" of food or money. It is also considered unlucky to sing carols outside the Christmas season.

Mistletoe: Mistletoe should be brought into the house on Christmas morning. Custom dictates that a gentleman may take a kiss from a girl standing under a sprig, on the condition that when doing so, he provides her with a berry plucked from it. Kisses must only be given and received as long as there are berries remaining on the sprig.

Thank You Very Much . . .

Dear [name of soon-to-be-ex husband],

Thank you so much for the dust buster/oven mitts/copy of How Clean Is Your House? It is so perceptive of you to realize that my burning ambition in life is to cater to your every need. A woman's place is, after all, in the kitchen, not at a fancy day spa or the opening night of an opera!

You may be wondering why I am writing you a thank-you note when we live in the same house. The fact is that we won't be for very much longer, and my lawyer has advised me to cease all verbal communication with you as of now. You will be hearing from him shortly. Merry Christmas!

Yours sincerely,

Things to Do
the Day After Christmas

The presents have been opened, a vast quantity of food has been consumed, and you're left with that post-Christmas feeling of anticlimax. What now? Perhaps consider the following:

❄ See a movie.

❄ Get to know all those wonderful gadgets you've been given and don't know how you've managed to live without. Read the manuals, insert batteries, and tinker away to your heart's content.

❄ If the shopaholic in you is still clamoring for more, hit the sales, snap up some bargains, and spend your gift cards.

❄ Go on a long winter walk to work off all those Christmas dinner calories.

❄ Organize a board game tournament. Choose four or five different games and play each one in turn for a set amount of time. Once that time is up, work out who was winning and award points for first place, second place, and so on. Then move on to the next game. The person with the most points at the end wins the title of Board Game King or Queen.

❄ Get the kids to write their thank you notes. Make it a fun activity rather than a chore by handing out blank cards, glue, scissors, paint, glitter, and stickers, and getting them to make their own. The personalized touch will be much appreciated by the recipients, too.

❄ Have a leftovers party and invite any friends and neighbors whom you weren't able to see on Christmas Day. The one rule is: absolutely no more cooking! Ask everyone to bring a dish of leftovers.

❄ Keep that Christmas spirit of goodwill alive and volunteer to do something for someone less fortunate than you. Homeless shelters in particular are always busy during the Christmas season and welcome volunteers.

❄ Pamper yourself for a day. Gather together all those beauty products you've been given, soak in a hot, scented bath, give yourself a manicure, slap on a face mask, and relax in front of the fire with a favorite book.

How to Pretend Christmas Isn't Happening

Year after year, you try your hardest to get into the spirit of Christmas. You struggle through crowds of hysterical last-minute shoppers; you throw out your back lugging home the biggest tree money can buy, only to find it doesn't fit in your living room; you arrange your features into an expression of wonder and delight when you unwrap this year's novelty tie featuring Donald Duck or Bart Simpson. But no matter how hard you try, you just can't cope with another Christmas. It's time to face the facts. You are one of life's Scrooges, and that's OK. Here are some suggested coping mechanisms:

❋ Convert to a religion that doesn't celebrate Christmas. Better still, make up your own religion.

❋ Embrace your Ebenezer tendencies! Wear severely cut, Victorian-style suits and walk around town with a sour expression on your face, shaking your cane and muttering at children or anyone else who looks like they might be having fun. Hire an impoverished yet goodhearted assistant and make him work long hours by candlelight while you sit counting your money on a pair of old-fashioned scales.

❄ Pretend that you are a moral campaigner, rather than the bitter old miser you are in reality, by loudly and argumentatively lecturing people about the evils of our consumer-led society and the cynical exploitation of the festive season.

❄ Make others feel guilty by proclaiming you are eschewing the frivolity of the season and instead will be spending Christmas volunteering in an African orphanage. Then draw the curtains, turn up the heat, and revel in the glory of a family-free, money-saving Yuletide.

❄ Hibernate.

It is, indeed, the season of regenerated feeling — the season for kindling, not merely the fire of hospitality in the hall, but the genial flame of charity in the heart.

— WASHINGTON IRVING

"Merry Christmas"
Around the World

Language	"Merry Christmas"	Pronunciation
ARABIC	عيد ميلاد سعيد	eid mee-lahd sah-eed
CATALAN	*Bon Nadal*	bon nad-ahl
CROATIAN	*Sretan Božić*	sre-than bau-zhee-ch
FRENCH	*Joyeux Noël*	Shwah-yuh no-el
GERMAN	*Fröhliche Weihnachten*	fruy-lic-ka vy-nack-ten

Language	"Merry Christmas"	Pronunciation
HINDI	क्रिस्मस की शुभ कामनाएं	christ-mas kee shubh kaam-naa-ye
HUNGARIAN	*Kellemes Karácsonyi ünnepeket*	kel-le-mesh ko-raa-thonji ew-ne-pe-ket
ITALIAN	*Buon Natale*	bwon nah-tah-lay
JAPANESE	メリークリスマス	me-rii ku-ri-su-ma-su
LATVIAN	*Priecīgus Ziemassvētkus*	preah-tsee-guhs zea-mahs-svat-kuhs
NORWEGIAN	*God Jul*	gord yule
POLISH	*Wesołych Świąt*	ve-so-wih shfyont
PORTUGUESE	*Feliz Natal*	fleej nut-ahl

Language	"Merry Christmas"	Pronunciation
ROMANIAN	*Crăcium Fericit*	crae-chun fer-ee-chit
SPANISH	*Feliz Navidad*	fay-leez nah-vee-dahd
TURKISH	*Noel'iniz kutlu olsun*	no-e-lee-neez koot-loo ol-soon
VIETNAMESE	*giáng sinh vui vẽ*	yan sin voo vay
WELSH	*Nadolig Llawen*	nahd-o-lig tlah-wen

Acknowledgments

Grateful thanks to First Edition Translations Limited, and Daniela Fava and Erika Kumzaite in particular, for providing the material on pages 109 to 111, and to David Woodroffe for providing the illustrations on page 17 and pages 82, 83, 84 (top) and 85.

Also Available . . .

Treat your family to something
AMAZING!

The **Family** Book

AMAZING THINGS TO DO **TOGETHER**

- OPTICAL ILLUSIONS AND MAGIC TRICKS
- MIND-BOGGLING PUZZLES AND RIDDLES
- UNIQUE ARTS AND CRAFTS

And more!

SCHOLASTIC

www.scholastic.com

FAMBOOK1

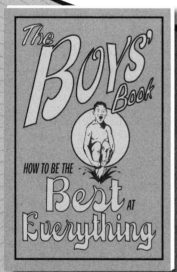

Every parent deserves
THE BEST!

FOR THE MOM WHO'S

- **Host the best parties!**
- **Get the kids to bed at night!**

FOR THE DAD WHO'S

- **Be the coolest dad on the block!**
- **Survive with your sanity!**